Terraces
&
Temples

JOHN ROBINSON

Terraces & Temples

THE CHOIR PRESS

First published in the United Kingdom in 2021 by
The Choir Press

ISBN 978-1-78963-230-9

Cover: Designed by John Robinson

For Mum and Dad

Contents

Birdsong	1
Gravity	2
Life on the wire	3
Oaknut	4
Llandudno	5
When the gardener has gone	6
Bench	7
The Donkey Stoners	8
Robin	9
Cloak	10
Snow on the roses	11
Little notes in second hand books	13
Chiromancy	14
Grandparents	15
Winter crown	16
The highest point on Earth	17
The apple tree	18
I still like to be beside the seaside	19
Fog	20
Memories of Rowarth	21
Joe	22
Murmurations	23
A shopping list for my daughter's future	24
The bridesmaid of Ancoats	25
On	27
Surrounded by trees	28
Physics	29
The bike and the coat	30

Lying awake at 3am worrying about heaven   31
Mind gardening   32
Winskill   33
Woodsmoke and whistling kettles   34
Looking for the red coat   35
Rock pools   37
Love letters   38
X-ray   39
The end of the season   40
Blackbirds in the goodnight   42

Birdsong

In the wood I sit and listen to birdsong
high up in the trees
one Robin's call echoes around
and is answered by another
and another
and another
they knit the tops of trees together
with audible string
guiding me with ancient sonar
back and forth
back and forth
weaving in and out of my heart
cocooning me in nature
shielding me from dark skies.

Gravity

Walking time worn paths
that disappear beneath my feet
not even bird song dares
to pierce this darkness.

The drapes of night
fall as velvet on a sleeping mind
sound is entombed
my senses have failed.

Across the heavens
there are no stars to guide me home
my compass is broken
my reality run aground.

I keep close that child's memory
of gold and silver days
when your laughter broke the water
and gravity let me go.

Life on the wire

Fly away little bird
from your life on the wire
through the heart of the town
and the sunset spire
across the emerald coast
and the Savannah plain
to a life in the sun
free from worry and pain.

Fly away little bird
from this deep winter's breath
where your bones won't be weighted
by the spectre of death
in a flock bound for heaven
you can wheel and soar
as the sun warms your heart
and the sea greets the shore.

Fly away little bird
hope we'll meet again soon
when the mercury rises
on a spring afternoon
I'll listen to your songs
born of love and desire
before the sun sets again
on your life on the wire.

Oaknut

As summer fell across the fields
I heard your laugh above the lark
my little oaknut grows so strong
your love it lifts my heavy heart.

In moments where I stand in awe
of what a gift you are to me
I'm haunted by what's yet to come
and what I might not live to see.

But selfish fears I cast aside
to sit and plant a dream with you
of all that you have yet to be
and all that you have yet to do.

And when I walk into the dusk
and your adventure's just begun
all those years of love will leave
new branches pointing at the sun.

Llandudno

Any time now I'll wake from this dream
and be there on the sands with you
the best dressed Mum in the whole of Llandudno
me in my orange vest.

Looking out to sea
I scrunched my eyes up tight
so that the sun on the water looked like a huge field of
diamonds
sparkling on a sheet of glass.

That year, at school I learnt that diamonds
are one of the hardest substances in nature
so I took one and used it to etch our names on the
moment.

As my eyes are relaxed
and the diamonds disappear
the sea rolls in to claim my heart.

I go back to my sandwiches
and you throw me one of those smiles.

When the gardener has gone

Over the bramble hedges and the old stone wall
there's a garden tucked away from the chaos of it all
where a man works the soil with tender, loving care
and swallows wheel and dive in the lucid summer air.

This garden is the empire of a gentle, loving man
a pair of battered wellies and an old watering can
to make the world a better place is his only goal
the flowers in the border are the colours of his soul.

A cat watches him working as it rests inside the shade
the robin looks for earthworms in the furrows that he's
made
all around him life ticks over but it's slightly out of time
bed sheets soak up sunshine on the morning washing
line.

Seasons roll through seasons and the days move us
along
and there will come a time when the gardener has gone
but the roses will still bloom and the sunflowers will
sway
and love is left behind that will never go away.

Bench

Cut from the eternals
the timeless fruits of Pan
laid across a laughter line
to commemorate a man
here I'll gaze upon the energy
of nature taking hold
reminded by the universe
that love cannot grow old.

The Donkey Stoners

At five to ten on Wednesdays past
milltown stone that shone like glass.

Twelve doors astride all nice and neat
plumes of gossip fill the street.

Rollers in and pinnys on
the Donkey Stoners, all for one.

Scrubbing to preserve their way
to keep one hand on yesterday.

Robin

September in the garden
wood smoke is heavy in the air
and the silence
is anesthetic for the soul.

Every incision I make
in the earth
brings you closer
worlds collide
and you appear
a glowing spark thrown from a fire.

Skipping over
freshly turned soil
you come to rest
on the handle of my spade
and my heart   *briefly*   *stops.*

One clumsy breath
and you're gone
your gentle bones
rising through dormant branches
into cold lifeless air.

I breathe again
ancient electricity
has passed through my heart
and I am reset.

Cloak

Weathered field and dry stone wall
hidden by a sleight of hand
so great that nature takes its bow
and drapes a cloak across the land.

Snow on the roses

I dream occasionally of that summer
when I waited in the rain
for the bus that called at your house
oh, to be sixteen again
sometimes it feels like the golden days
were only passing through
there's snow on the roses
but I still love you.

It's cold today darling
though the ice has been and gone
aches and pains to be expected
now we're eighty winters on
and yet when I look into your eyes
I can't help but feel new
there's snow on the roses
but I still love you.

But we're entering the twilight
the parts hidden by the frame
time shows no mercy
tears hold no shame
we're looking through life's telescope
at a disappearing view
there's snow on the roses
but I still love you.

I wouldn't change a second of this
it's largely been a blast
one day we'll walk in sunshine
and perfect shadows will be cast
for now I'll stick the kettle on
and make another brew
there's snow on the roses
but I still love you.

Little notes in second hand books

"To Jonathan, Christmas 78"
from Uncle Frank, who was always late
in his gabardine mac and trilby hat
jazz whistling while he fed the cat.

"To Suzy, Christmas 81"
from Mrs. Dudley long since gone
big bloomers out on washing day
a purple rinse to hide the grey.

"To Richard, Christmas 86"
from all the gang at number six
bloodied knees, short back and sides
rainy seaside donkey rides.

To all of those who have been and gone
a distant memory designed
little notes in second hand books
a piece of love that's left behind.

Chiromancy

The day lies draped
across wire hedgerows
fistfuls of black cloud
choke the sky.

Streams are muted
crystalline and cracked
fractures bow and bend.

Faces lie distorted
in the mirror's ice
and flicker in the whiteout.

A murder of crows
fix stares to empty horizons.

Lines drift and disappear
out of the hands of fortune.

Grandparents

The world famous Sunday roast
the postcards from the sunshine coast
the arms that always held you close
Grandparents.

The prehistoric motor car
the just nipped out, but never far
the overflowing biscuit jar
Grandparents.

The Christmas gifts that were just too small
the sunlight on the bedroom wall
the feeling you were eight foot tall
Grandparents.

The Thermos on the windswept hill
the little box with the little pill
the laughter that somehow hangs there still
Grandparents.

The dictionary of yesteryear
the gentle sound on a youthful ear
the words that kept away the fear
Grandparents.

The fire that's lying in the grate
the last few moments holding fate
the love that goes on being great
Grandparents.

Winter crown

At dreaming time
snow lands gently on silent lanes
like Pegasus descending.

At dawn's break
footprints become a secret code
rooks blink in the sky like binary.

The air is spiked with ice
words turn to ghosts
and mourn the dying sun.

Bring the forest to the mantel
grab a glass and light the fire
the lips of the year are growing thin.

Pink skies and night falls
a kingdom sighs
and reaches for it's winter crown.

The highest point on Earth

I've never been the adventurous type
I once got lost in my eiderdown looking for a lost
civilisation
made myself sick with Kendal mint cake
took a dinghy out on a raging canal … and sank it
mouth full of old shopping trolleys and lolly sticks.

But when you told me you loved me
I became Clark Kent with a convincing disguise
Indiana Jones with a better hat
a Bond that opens doors for old ladies.

Now I spend my days admiring the view
from the highest point on Earth.

The apple tree

When yesterday was just a lad
and swifts turned tail in gold sunshine
we planted up an apple tree
a link between your heart and mine.

And through sharp frosts and driving rain
and bluebells pushing through the snow
you watched the seasons slowly turn
and quietly I watched you grow.

And loved ones came and loved ones went
old sailing ships on distant seas
and still the tree bore happy fruit
a resting place for birds and bees.

And freckle flecked and kind of heart
your soul it grew like woodland pine
the apple tree constant and bright
gave life back to my troubled mind.

Now when you talk with blazing eyes
of summer skies and widescreen dreams
your spark of life ignites my bones
and I understand what all this means.

So raise a toast to the apple tree
and Eden's gracious, golden sun
to celebrate the days we've shared
and all the love that's yet to come.

I still like to be beside the seaside

When time threatens to weather me
and lights warn that rocks are near
I can be that child again
when my soul drops anchor here.

Fog

It descends
and the land becomes flat
simplified into two dimensions
a deserted puppet theatre
an empty popup book
no buildings
no angles
no symmetry
no design
vistas untouched by brutal egos.

This is nature showing her hand
her power to slowly strip away
everything we create.

This land
is now ruled by the tree
ash, oak and willow
branches like drops of oil displaced in water
stab out at a missing sky.

Waiting for the flicker of early sodium
we throw lights into the distance
looking for a way through the confusion
looking for a clear road home.

Memories of Rowarth

Grandma's tomato sandwiches
as wet as the stream we paddled in.

Dragonflies like clockwork toys
casting a blue haze over the water.

Sunday trousers rolled up to the knees
a garland of wildflowers for Mum.

Letting the afternoon slip gently away
Grandad filling his pipe and ruffling my hair.

Wondering where the stream began
and where love would take us.

Joe

In those precious moments when a new day is born
the corporation sun met the rising dawn
a murder of crows wheeled away in retreat
as Joe dragged his cart down Chadwick Street.

One of life's boxers Joe had taken the blows
his face a map of somewhere that no one ever goes
exchanging the past for soap and stones
patchwork rags on lifeless bones.

Old women would smile at the mention of his name
gathering around him like moths to a flame
birthdays and Christmases gathered up and sold
destined for the tin and never for the gold.

I was just a young boy but I saw it in his eyes
Joe was one of us without the intricate disguise
he looked into the mirrors ice and felt the fresh decay
knowing that his time was ebbing silently away.

Eventually Joe's cart would turn to ashes on the fire
his memory was snagged in the thorns on the brier
the murder circled wildly in a dark sky of sleet
as a long black car drove down Chadwick Street.

Joe had been a part of life since I was really small
every week I heard the gravel in his clarion call
some memories return to dust, some get etched in stone
the first words of this babe in arms?
"Mummy ... rag and bone!"

Murmurations

And then my thoughts take flight
soaring over black terrace slate
worry and fear twisting overhead
blocking out the milk glass sun.

Patterns form that seem strangely familiar
returning to test my reality
the dark symphony of an orchestra
being conducted from behind a hidden curtain.

I need a solitary predator
to carry each one away
but the sky is full of black noise.

Daylight is beginning to fade
and the thoughts continue
until with one last sweeping motion
they roost themselves away
where dust gathers
in my darkness.

A shopping list for my daughter's future

1 x distant star to guide you home
2 x hearts so you're never alone
1 x endless horizon
1 x pearlescent sea
1 x home filled with love and your very own key
1 x glorious sunset after a storm
1 x late summer breeze to keep memories warm
1 x climbable mountain
1 x breachable wall
1 x beautiful soul who will give you it all
1 x love for all people under the sun
1 x songbird to tell you the day has begun
1 x deep valley sunrise
1 x pocket of rays
1 x long endless rainbow to colour your days

The bridesmaid of Ancoats

In that biscuit tin
love's forgotten children
are kept alive
by the DNA of old fingers
and an ochre sun.

Open the lid and
they flicker into life
hickory dock stares
hand me down smiles
broken shadows.

She'd flick through those memories
selecting her favourites
cherry picking time and
placing days in order of reverence
a game of top trumps
won by the hand of melancholy.

Gathering shells in Southport
Whit week walks in the Goyt valley
The bridesmaid of Ancoats
The best of times.

Lingering sadness was
skimmed away
on distant shorelines.

She prayed for early morning mist
for easter psalms and sunlit piers
ring the bells for terraces and temples
and love's forgotten children.

On

You're gone now
taken by a man made sun
blistering heat
has returned you to ash.

There was no violence
to your passing
in the end
you went happily
baptised by the warmth
of a higher power.

Your laughter is still here
soldered to the air
your name is written
on the gossamer
of butterflies and bees.

Although I can't see it from here
I still hear the river flowing
behind the trees
dependable and cyclical
you go on.

Surrounded by trees

The freight on the hillside
time marches on
the wheels of life turn
tomorrow they're gone
there's just you and me now
under rag cotton skies
watching over Pen-y
with larks on the rise.

Guarded by bluebells
and branches of thorn
into the wood
forever reborn
we live on in the bird song
high notes on the breeze
back to the earth
surrounded by trees.

Physics

Watching the telly
Gran would stare open mouthed
as the magician passed his hand
through a solid object.

Secondary school physics would have
explained how it wasn't possible
but I kept quiet and left her to the magic.

Thirty years later and through the windows of the care
home
Mum would blow me a parting kiss
and I'd feel it travelling through the glass
and landing on my cheek.

On the way home
abandoning logic
I'd touch my face and smile.

Physics was never my strongest subject.

The bike and the coat

My role has altered, my life has changed
I sit on park benches watching other people's games
I'm your Dad and I'll be sat over there
with the bike you don't ride
and the coat you won't wear.

My position is clear, my vocation complete
I'm the old guy who carries your stuff down the street
but I'm still your Dad so I'll be sat over there
with the bike you don't ride
and the coat you won't wear.

I'm an ageing packhorse with worn out shoes
carrying around a bad case of the blues
but I'm still your Dad and I'll be sat over there
with the bike you don't ride
and the coat you won't wear.

Your life has just begun, destination love
stare out at the oceans and the heavens above
in case of heartbreak I'll be sat over there
with the bike you don't ride
and the coat you won't wear.

Life's a brittle kingdom, you'll rise and you'll fall
while trying to understand your place in it all
when you need me just holler I'll always be there
with the bike you don't ride
and the coat you won't wear.

Lying awake at 3am worrying about heaven

If I die wearing my scruffs
will they let me into heaven?
will they refuse entry to their club
if it's gone half past eleven?

Will St. Peter ask me where I'm from
and will he like my answer?
or will he turn me away if I'm under age
suspecting that I'm a chancer?

If I perish while in a motor car
will I have to pay to park?
will the car be safe at the cemetery gates
even after dark?

If the ghosts of traffic wardens
spot my car on yellow lines
will I have to spend eternity
paying off their fines?

Still awake at 4:30am …

If I'm old and immobile when I die
and there really are three steps to heaven
do you think they'll have wheelchair access?

Mind gardening

I've neglected it recently
but in my garden there's a little patch of shade
where I'm trying to grow some flowers
so you'll have something nice to look at
when you step inside.

Winskill

Sometimes silence becomes a wall
that stretches way beyond my understanding
I'm in the healing place
where time has no value
and beauty can't be measured
by instruments of skin and bone.

Worry lives outside
this cotton framed stage
as we turn full circle
struggling to express our wonder
nature holds us majestically to its beating heart
and all is well
a mother meets her child
for the first time.

Larks take flight
casting shadows over pasture
words are broken
don't speak
the air is full.

Woodsmoke and whistling kettles

On the towpath a sharp line of trees
appear in nature's mirror
torched with copper and bronze
reflections bend and break.

Fruit falls from the sycamore
and heads downstream
crossing watery paths
with mallard and moorhen.

Emma sits under the oak
the scent of summer is gone
and the marigolds on her deck are dying back
she's in need of fresh paint
a new winter coat.

Woodsmoke and whistling kettles
horses in the meadow
geese on the bank.

There's a gentle hum from overhead wires
and for a moment
we're reminded that worlds exist
beyond this one.

Looking for the red coat

It was Christmas 1980
when he hung up the red coat
and the penny dropped.

The signs had been there for a while
I had a few questions
so I made a list:

You can't really have a white beard and ginger sideburns,
can you?
We have a gas fire, how does the chimney thing work?
Can anyone really explain what omnipresence is?

That Christmas I asked for world peace
just to see what happened
and I got an Action Man instead
the game was up.

And yet every Christmas
I still catch a flash of red
out of the corner of my eye
candle flames bend with promise
an extra layer of soot forms on the hearth.

It's in those moments
that I reach out for the child
who believed in love and magic.

On the dark winter streets of the past
he's still out there
walking through neon lit snow
looking for the red coat.

Rock pools

Somehow you still exist
in calico afternoons
lights and motors and electricity
have reanimated your memory.

In this world filled with dust and scratches
I watch you wandering across the beach
gazing into rock pools
young and carefree.

Pausing the film
I stare straight into your eyes
looking for a way into the past
but I'm staring through a tiny crack
in a door that can't be opened.

Hitting play again
the sea comes in
the rock pools empty
and you begin to move silently
out of the frame.

Love letters

The light that fell across your face
and had me making plans
it only fell that way once.

The gulls that cried on the deserted pier
as we pinched each other's chips
they only cried that way once.

The rude joke I told in the promenade cafe
that made you spill your tea
I only told it once.

***

Empty shells on endless sands
bleached by a hundred suns.

Memories offered to the sea
the day was never ours to keep.

X-ray

The still
the ice
a frozen stream with worlds
that are unreachable
until radiation
opens the scar.

From a bedroom window
trees shake
in an easterly wind
branches
are elevated
broken
and repositioned
birds fight the air
with all that's left of grace.

Hope travels
through bone
and we pray
for the sun
to bring kinder shadows.

The end of the season

There's gorse on the hedgerow
on the coast of a dream
where the foxgloves sway
and the gulls spin and scream
in moments before sleep
I'm back there on the prom
but it's the end of the season
and the fairground has gone.

I remember your faces
and how at home you were there
how the sea washed away
all your worry and care
ice creams, penny fountains
and seafront cafes
they were simple and carefree
those dandelion days.

I'd love to say thank you
for those laughs by the sea
share a quick bag of chips
and a weak flask of tea
but you've sailed out of sight
on a disappeared coast
and my memories are fading
like a traveller's ghost

Now I hope that you've found
a seafront in between
the world that we know
and the worlds that aren't seen
I've spent up on the slots
and I'm alone on the prom
it's the end of the season
and the fairground has gone.

Blackbirds in the goodnight

It's the golden hour
and I hear older children
playing in the street outside
swearing, bouncing balls on flagstones
riding bikes.

Fighting sleep
I make faces from old patterned curtains
but my eyelids are heavy
and starting to fall.

In these last few minutes
blackbirds sing to each other
across oak and ash and sycamore
stitching a quilted sky together with melody
and gently tucking in the sun.

I smell the scent of dreaming time
warm roses on castle walls.

The fight is over and I go gently
grateful for today
hopeful for tomorrow.